The ANCIENT MESOPOTAMIANS

MYTHS *of the* WORLD

THE ANCIENT MESOPOTAMIANS

VIRGINIA SCHOMP

mc **Marshall Cavendish**
Benchmark
New York

∼ For Katherine Truesdell ∼

The author would like to thank Benjamin R. Foster,
Laffan Professor of Assyriology and Babylonian Literature, Yale University,
for his valuable comments and careful reading of the manuscript.

Benchmark Books Marshall Cavendish 99 White Plains Road Tarrytown, New York 10591 www.marshall-cavendish.com Text copyright © 2009 by Marshall Cavendish Corporation All rights reserved. No part of this book may be reproduced or utilized in any form or by any means electronic or mechanical, including photocopying, recording, or by any information storage and retrieval system, without permission from the copyright holders. All Internet sites were available and accurate when this book was sent to press. LIBRARY OF CONGRESS CATALOGING-IN-PUBLICATION DATA Schomp, Virginia. The ancient Mesopotamians / by Virginia Schomp. p. cm. — (Myths of the world) Summary: "A retelling of several major ancient Mesopotamian myths, with background information describing the history, geography, belief systems, and customs of Mesopotamia"--Provided by publisher. Includes bibliographical references and index. ISBN 978-0-7614-3095-7 1. Mythology, Assyro-Babylonian—Juvenile literature. 2. Civilization, Assyro-Babylonian—Juvenile literature. I. Title. BL1620.S34 2008 299'.21—dc22 2008007052

EDITOR: Joyce Stanton ART DIRECTOR: Anahid Hamparian
PUBLISHER: Michelle Bisson SERIES DESIGNER: Michael Nelson

Images provided by Rose Corbett Gordon and Alexandra (Sasha) Gordon, Art Editors of Mystic CT, from the following sources: Cover: The Art Archive/Private Collection Back cover: The Art Archive/Archaeological Museum Istanbul/Gianni Dagli Orti Page 1, 45: Scala/Art Resource, NY; pages 2-3, 30-31, 38, 46, 48, 62, 64, 67, 80, 81, 82, 86 center, 87 top: Mary Evans Picture Library/The Image Works; pages 6, 22, 26: The Art Archive/Musée du Louvre Paris/Gianni Dagli Orti; pages 7, 19, 85: The Granger Collection, NY; page 8: The Art Archive/Archaeological Museum Aleppo Syria/Gianni Dagli Orti; pages 10-11: British Museum/Boltin Picture Library/The Bridgeman Art Library; page 12: The Art Archive/Musée du Louvre Paris/Gianni Dagli Orti; page 15: Sotheby's/akg-images; pages 16, 32, 34: The Print Collector/Heritage-Images/The Image Works; pages 18, 72: British Museum/Art Resource, NY; page 20: The Art Archive/Private Collection; page 23: Louvre, Paris, France/Giraudon/The Bridgeman Art Library; page 24: National Museum, Aleppo, Syria/Giraudon/The Bridgeman Art Library; page 27: National Museum, Damascus, Syria/Giraudon/The Bridgeman Art Library; page 29: ET Archive, London/SuperStock; page 36: The Art Archive/Archaeological Museum Istanbul/Gianni Dagli Orti; pages 37, 52, 57, 74, 76, 87 bottom: Erich Lessing/Art Resource, NY; pages 40, 42: The Art Archive/British Museum/Alfredo Dagli Orti; pages 49, 60: The Art Archive/National Museum Damascus Syria/Gianni Dagli Orti; page 50: Werner Forman/British Museum/The Image Works; pages 54, 56, 86 bottom: Louvre/The Bridgeman Art Library; page 69: Werner Forman Archive/Iraq Museum Baghdad/The Image Works; page 70: AAAC/Topham/The Image Works; page 71: Silvio Fiore/SuperStock; page 86 top: The Detroit Institute of Arts, Founders Society purchase, General Membership Fund/The Bridgeman Art Library; page 89: British Museum/The Bridgeman Art Library.

Front cover: The warrior-kings of Mesopotamia's Assyrian Empire were regarded as special mortals whose power and authority came from the gods.
Half-title page: A gold bull's head decorates a musical instrument discovered in an ancient Mesopotamian tomb.
Title page: After many hardships and dangers, the epic hero Gilgamesh discovers the plant of eternal life.
Back cover: A snarling lion prowls across a wall in ancient Babylon.

CONTENTS

THE MAGIC *of* MYTHS

EVERY ANCIENT CULTURE HAD ITS MYTHS. These timeless tales of gods and heroes give us a window into the beliefs, values, and practices of people who lived long ago. They can make us think about the BIG QUESTIONS that have confronted humankind down through the ages: questions about human nature, the meaning of life, and what happens after death. On top of all that, myths are simply great stories that are lots of fun to read.

Above: An ancient Mesopotamian god, part human, part animal, sculpted around four thousand years ago

What makes a story a myth? Unlike a narrative written by a particular author, a myth is a traditional story that has been handed down from generation to generation, first orally and later in written form. Nearly all myths tell the deeds of gods, goddesses, and other divine beings. These age-old tales were once widely accepted as true and sacred. Their primary purpose was to explain the mysteries of life and the origins of a society's customs, institutions, and religious rituals.

It is sometimes hard to tell the difference between a myth and a heroic legend. Both myths and legends are traditional stories that may include extraordinary elements such as gods, spirits, magic, and monsters. Both may be partly based on real events in the distant past. However, the main characters in legends are usually mortals rather than divine beings. Another key difference is that legends are basically exciting action stories, while myths almost always express deeper meanings or truths.

Mythology (the whole collection of myths belonging to a society) played an important role in ancient cultures. In very early times, people created myths to explain the awe-inspiring, uncontrollable forces of nature, such as thunder, lightning, darkness, drought, and death. Even after science began to develop more rational explanations for these mysteries, myths continued to provide comforting answers to the many questions that could never be fully resolved. People of nearly all cultures have asked the same basic questions about the world around them. That is why myths from different times and places can be surprisingly similar. For example, the peoples of almost every ancient culture told stories about the creation of the world, the origins of gods and humans, the changing of the seasons, and the afterlife.

Hammurabi was the founder of Mesopotamia's mighty Babylonian Empire.

Sacrificial rituals were part of nearly all ancient cultures. In this ancient Mesopotamian wall painting, a priest leads a bull to an altar where it will be offered up to the gods.

Mythology served ancient cultures as instruction, inspiration, and entertainment. It offered a way for the people of a society to express their fundamental beliefs and values and pass them down to future generations. It helped preserve memories of their civilization's past glories and held up examples of ideal human qualities and conduct. Finally, these imaginative stories provided enjoyment to countless listeners and readers in ancient times, just as they do today.

The MYTHS OF THE WORLD series explores the mythology of some of history's greatest civilizations. Each book opens with a brief look at the culture that created the myths, including its geographical setting, political history, government, society, and religious beliefs. Next comes the fun part: the stories themselves. We have based our retellings of the myths selected for these books on a variety of traditional sources. The new versions are fun and easy to read. At the same time, we have strived to remain true to the spirit of the ancient tales, preserving their magic, their mystery, and the special ways of speech and avenues of thought that made each culture unique.

As you read the myths, you will come across sidebars, or text boxes, highlighting topics related to each story's characters or themes. The sidebars in *The Ancient Mesopotamians* include excerpts from ancient hymns and narrative poems. The sources for the excerpts are explained in the Notes on Quotations on page 90. You'll find lots of other useful material at the back of the book as well, including information on ancient Mesopotamian writing and texts, a glossary of difficult terms, suggestions for further reading, and more. Finally, the stories are illustrated with both ancient and modern sculptures, paintings, and other works of art inspired by mythology. These images can help us better understand the spirit of the myths and the way a society's traditional tales have influenced other cultures through the ages.

Now it is time to begin our adventures in ancient Mesopotamia. We hope that you will enjoy this journey to a land where mysterious gods and goddesses watch over the heavens and earth, cities and temples, fertile fields and life-giving waters. Most of all, we hope that the sampling of stories and art in this book will inspire you to further explorations of the magical world of mythology.

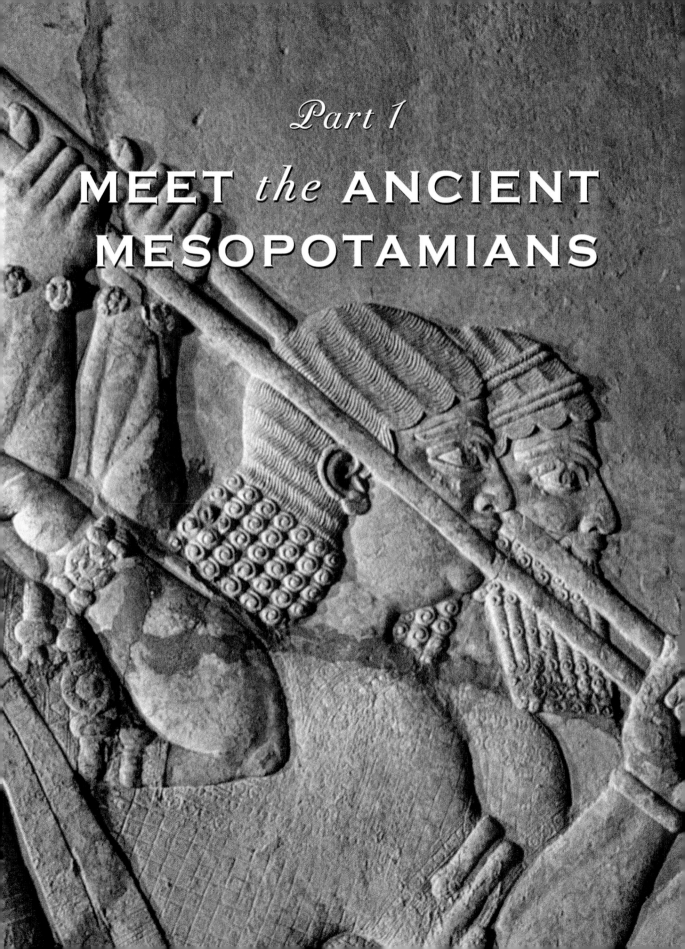

Part 1
MEET *the* ANCIENT MESOPOTAMIANS

The LAND BETWEEN THE RIVERS

ANCIENT MESOPOTAMIA LAY BETWEEN THE TIGRIS AND Euphrates rivers, in roughly the same area as modern-day Iraq. The climate in Mesopotamia was hot and dry. Without the rivers, the land would have been a bleak desert. Each spring the Tigris and Euphrates swelled with rain and melted snow from mountains to the north. The rivers overflowed their banks, flooding the surrounding plains. When the waters receded, they left behind a layer of rich black silt. More than four thousand years ago, the people of the region developed a system of canals to bring water from the rivers to this fertile soil. Their sophisticated irrigation system turned Mesopotamia into one of the ancient world's richest agricultural regions.

The same rivers that brought life could take it away. Some years the waters rose too high, unleashing violent floods that wiped out entire communities. At other times the spring floods were poor, and the season's crops failed. The people of Mesopotamia also had to contend

Opposite: The Mesopotamians traveled the rivers in sturdy boats made from wood, reeds, or animal hides.

Previous page: Assyrian king Assurbanipal and his attendants take part in a lion hunt.

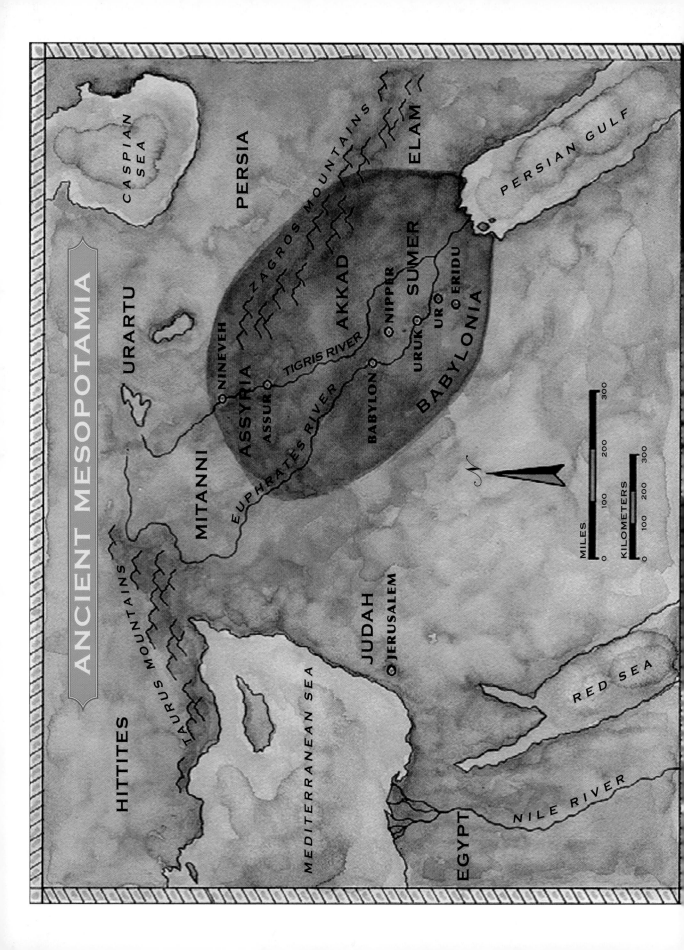

with destructive sandstorms, swarms of locusts, and diseases that destroyed plants and livestock. They had to labor constantly to build and maintain their canals. In addition, irrigation waters carried salts that settled in the soil. Over time the salted fields yielded fewer and fewer crops. Farmers eventually were forced to abandon their fields and search for more fertile land.

All these hardships shaped the ancient Mesopotamians' view of their place in the world. Like the forces of nature, the gods were seen as mysterious, powerful, and unpredictable, bringing life one day and destruction the next. The role of human beings was to serve the gods and submit to their will. In "The Rebellion of the Gods" on page 41, we will learn how the gods made the first men and women to relieve themselves of the burden of labor.

Nineveh, on the east bank of the Tigris River, was one of the most splendid cities of the ancient world. Its ruins, painted here by the nineteenth-century artist William Turner, are part of the modern city of Mosul in Iraq.

CRADLE *of* CIVILIZATION

*T*HE FIRST FARMING VILLAGES GREW UP BETWEEN THE Tigris and Euphrates rivers more than seven thousand years ago. As the people of these early settlements prospered and multiplied, their small villages developed into thriving towns. Migrants came from neighboring lands to share in the prosperity. Around 3500 BCE, in an area of southern Mesopotamia known as Sumer, these mingled groups of people laid the foundations for the world's first civilization.

The Sumerians built the first-ever cities. They developed organized government, law, and religion. They made remarkable advances in science, mathematics, and technology. They also invented the world's first writing system. Because of their many accomplishments, Mesopotamia is often called the cradle of civilization.

Ancient Sumer was not a united nation. Instead, it was a land of independent city-states, each consisting of a large city and the farms and villages surrounding it. Around 2330 BCE, the divided city-states

Opposite: Sargon was the first king to unite all of Mesopotamia under a single ruler.

Carved bulls march across the outer wall of a temple near the ancient Sumerian city of Ur.

were conquered by Sargon, king of Akkad, a region in the north. Sargon united northern and southern Mesopotamia, forming the world's first empire.

After Sargon's death his empire fell apart. Over the following centuries, Mesopotamia was home to a series of different civilizations. Among them were two of the ancient world's greatest empires, Babylonia and Assyria.

The founder of the Babylonian Empire was Hammurabi. This warrior-king took the throne of the southern city-state of Babylon in 1792 BCE. Within a few years, he had built his small city into the capital of a reunited Mesopotamia. As ruler of the Babylonian Empire, Hammurabi set down one of the ancient world's most famous codes of laws. In the prologue to the Code of Hammurabi, the king proclaimed that he had been called by the gods "to show forth justice in the land, to destroy the evil and wicked, to ensure that the powerful not oppress the weak, to rise like the sun-god . . . to give light to the land."

Under the rulers who followed Hammurabi, the Babylonian Empire was torn apart by civil wars and famine. In the fourteenth century BCE, the northern kingdom of Assyria took Mesopotamia to new heights of power and glory. The Assyrians were fierce warriors who built the largest empire the world had ever seen, stretching from Persia (present-day Iran) to Egypt. Assurbanipal, one of the last great Assyrian kings, assembled a huge library in his palace at Nineveh. Several of the myths in this book are based partly on ancient texts discovered in the ruins of Assurbanipal's library.

Soon after Assurbanipal's death in 627 BCE, the Assyrian Empire toppled. For a brief time, Babylon regained its former glory. The best-known ruler of the New Babylonian Empire was Nebuchadrezzar II. The Bible portrays Nebuchadrezzar as the brutal conqueror who destroyed Jerusalem in 586 BCE and carried the Hebrew people into exile. Ancient Babylonian texts celebrate him for restoring Babylon's power, wealth, and splendor.

In 539 BCE Babylon fell to the Persian Empire. That brought an end to nearly three thousand years of political independence for Mesopotamia. But the glories of the region's great civilizations did not die. Ancient peoples including the Hebrews, Greeks, and Romans would carry Mesopotamian culture and mythology throughout the world.

The Babylonian king Hammurabi is remembered mainly for his famous code of laws.

A variety of systems of dating have been used by different cultures throughout history. Many historians now prefer to use BCE (Before Common Era) and CE (Common Era) instead of BC (Before Christ) and AD (Anno Domini), out of respect for the diversity of the world's peoples.

GOVERNMENT *and* SOCIETY

THE CIVILIZATIONS OF ANCIENT MESOPOTAMIA WERE ruled by warrior-kings. Kings were regarded as extraordinary mortals chosen by the gods to serve as their representatives on earth. That sacred role brought important duties. As the royal patron of the state religion, the king was responsible for building temples and performing rituals to honor the gods. He was expected to expand his territories through conquests that enriched the kingdom and glorified the gods. He also had to maintain the roads and irrigation canals and promote law and justice.

A vast network of government officials helped the king carry out his many duties. High-ranking officials such as royal counselors and territorial governors belonged to Mesopotamia's rich and powerful upper class. The upper class also included princes and other royal relatives, leading priests, and top military officers.

The middle class was made up of many lower-ranking government

Opposite: Amid a grand display of wealth and power, an Assyrian king returns to his capital.

officials and priests, as well as most merchants, craftspeople, soldiers, and scribes. Scribes kept official records, wrote out business letters, and performed other writing tasks for a living.

Farmers were ranked near the bottom of the social scale. Most farmers labored in fields belonging to the temples, kings, or other rich landowners. Mesopotamian farm tools included the ox-drawn plow, the sickle (a cutting tool with a curved blade), and a type of short-handled hoe called a pickax.

Slaves belonged to the lowest class in Mesopotamian society. Some slaves were foreigners captured in war. Others were native-born men, women, and children who had been sold into slavery to pay their debts. The majority of slaves worked as household servants or farmhands.

Two laborers at work, in a wall carving from the palace of an Assyrian king

The women of ancient Mesopotamia shared the social status of their fathers or husbands. However, women did not have the same legal rights as men. In Assyria especially, the laws made the husband the undisputed head of the household. A man had the right to beat his wife for a wide variety of offenses, such as leaving the house without permission or appearing in public without a veil.

Despite these restrictions, some women managed to move beyond their traditional roles as wives, mothers, and homemakers. Middle-class women might participate in their husbands' businesses or work as midwives, brewers, or tavern keepers. Upper-class women often enjoyed considerable political or economic power.

A Sumerian princess clasps her hands in prayer.

Some wealthy young women became scribes or priestesses. A priestess spent her life at a temple, serving the gods and goddesses and praying for her family. Enheduanna, daughter of the Sumerian king Sargon, was high priestess to Inanna, goddess of love, fertility, and war. More than four thousand years ago, the priestess composed a set of hymns to Inanna. In one hymn she identified herself by name, becoming the world's first known author:

> En-hedu-anna am I, I will now say a prayer to you.
> My tears, like sweet beer
> I now shed freely for you, fate-determining Inanna.

GODS *and* DEMONS

THE ANCIENT MESOPOTAMIANS BELIEVED IN HUNDREDS of gods, goddesses, and other supernatural beings. At the top of this divine assembly were three creator gods: An (or Anu), god of the heavens; Enlil (or Ellil), god of the earth; and Enki (or Ea), god of the waters and wisdom. In late Sumerian times, Enlil was honored as supreme ruler of all the gods. The Babylonians gave that exalted role to their national god, Marduk, while the chief Assyrian god was Assur. The two most important female deities were Ninhursag (also known as Nintu or Damkina), goddess of birth and motherhood, and Inanna (or Ishtar), goddess of love, fertility, and war.

Along with these chief gods and goddesses, the spirit world included a host of lesser deities. There were gods of the sun, moon, fields, farms, rivers, mountains, and other aspects of nature. There were gods associated with human institutions such as hunting and brick making. There were even deities in charge of the humble plow

Opposite: A statue of an unknown goddess holding a vessel, discovered in the ruins of a temple on the Euphrates River

One of the many fantastic creatures found in Mesopotamian mythology, this deity combines the head of a man with the body of a four-legged winged beast.

and pickax. All of these mighty beings were immortal, and they had extraordinary powers. At the same time, they often looked and acted much like ordinary mortals. They ate, drank, slept, and felt love, joy, sorrow, anger, and other human emotions.

The spirit world was also home to a host of dangerous ghosts and demons. The ghosts of people who had not received a proper burial could avenge themselves on the living. Evil demons brought disease, death, and other misfortunes.

The Mesopotamians believed that a person's body and spirit separated after death. The spirit lived on below the earth in the Land of No Return. This vast and gloomy kingdom was ruled by Ereshkigal, sister of the goddess Inanna. In "Inanna Descends to the Underworld" (page 63), the goddess makes a decidedly unpleasant visit to her sister's dark realm.

THE GODS *and* GODDESSES *of* MESOPOTAMIA

The ancient Mesopotamians practiced a complex religion with hundreds of different deities. Here are a few of their most important gods and goddesses.

AN God of the heavens; also known as Anu

ENLIL God of the earth; also known as Ellil

ENKI God of the waters and wisdom; also known as Ea

MARDUK Chief god of Babylon

NINHURSAG Goddess of birth and motherhood; also known as Nintu or Damkina

INANNA Goddess of love, fertility, and war; also known as Ishtar

DUMUZI God of vegetation and fertility; also known as Tammuz

APSU God of freshwater

TIAMAT Goddess of salt water

ANSHAR God of the horizon

KISHAR Goddess of the horizon

ERESHKIGAL Queen of the underworld

The goddess Inanna

SERVANTS *of* THE GODS

WHEN THE GODS WERE CONTENTED, THEY BLESSED THE people with prosperity. When they were angry, disasters such as famine, disease, and devastating floods could follow. Every Mesopotamian, from the king down to the lowliest farm laborer, worked hard to stay on the good side of these all-powerful beings.

Kings honored the gods by building and maintaining the temples. Some cities had magnificent mud-brick temple-towers known as ziggurats. A ziggurat had several stepped platforms connected by outside staircases, leading to a shrine at the top. The city's patron god lived in the temple's inner sanctuary in the form of a holy statue.

Priests performed daily rituals to make sure the gods were happy in their earthly homes. They offered hymns of praise and animal sacrifices. They bathed, dressed, and fed the divine statues. One Sumerian text listed the foods placed in the inner sanctuary of a temple each day. The menu included more than forty sheep, eight lambs, seventy birds,

and fifty-four containers of wine and beer. The "leftovers" from this divine feast went to the king or the temple staff.

The pyramid-shaped ziggurat is the tallest building in this fanciful painting of an ancient Assyrian city.

Ordinary people adopted "personal gods" as their special protectors. Every home had a small shrine, where the family presented prayers and offerings to their chosen gods. The personal gods acted as "middlemen," carrying the family's requests to the gods at the top of the divine order.

On special occasions the entire community joined together in worship. The greatest religious celebration of the Babylonian era was the New Year's Festival. This grand event celebrated the renewal of life each spring. It featured prayers, rituals, and sacrifices. Priests paraded the holy images of Marduk and other gods through the streets of Babylon. They also recited *Enuma Elish*, the sacred story of the creation of the world and the birth of the gods.

Part 2

TIMELESS TALES *of* ANCIENT MESOPOTAMIA

THE ORIGINS *of the* WORLD *and the* GODS

"When on High"

ACCORDING TO A BABYLONIAN MYTH, THE WORLD began when Marduk, king of the gods, separated heaven and earth. The ancient poem known as *Enuma Elish* tells this creation story. The title of the poem comes from its opening words, which mean, "when on high."

Enuma Elish recalls a time when the universe was nothing but water. The freshwater was a god named Apsu, and the salt water was the goddess Tiamat. From their union new gods were born. Eventually the younger generation of gods, led by Marduk, overthrew their elders. Marduk formed the earth and sky from Tiamat's body. Then he established a new order in the world, with each god assigned to a particular role and himself as king.

This Babylonian creation story celebrates the beginnings of kingship and government. It also glorifies Marduk as the most powerful of all the gods. Each year priests in Babylon recited and acted out *Enuma*

Opposite: Tiamat appears as a monster in later depictions of the Babylonian creation story.

Previous page: The hero Gilgamesh passes through a beautiful garden on his quest for immortality.

Elish as part of the New Year's Festival. Through their sacred ceremonies, they hoped to persuade Marduk to grant the people a year of peace and prosperity.

CAST *of* CHARACTERS

Apsu (AHP-soo) God of freshwater
Tiamat (tee-AH-maht) Goddess of salt water
Anshar (AHN-shahr) God of the horizon; father of An
Kishar (KIH-shahr) Goddess of the horizon; mother of An
An (ahn) God of the heavens
Enki (EN-kee) God of the waters and wisdom
Mummu (MUH-moo) Apsu's vizier, or chief adviser
Damkina (DAM-kih-nah) Goddess of birth and motherhood; wife of Enki
Marduk (MAR-duk) Son of Enki; chief god of Babylon
Kingu (KIN-goo) Chief commander of Tiamat's forces
Enlil (EN-lil) God of the earth

WHEN ON HIGH THERE WERE NO HEAVENS, when below there was no earth, then all alone in the universe were Apsu and Tiamat. Apsu's body was the sweet freshwater. Tiamat was the tumultuous sea.

Over long ages the sweet and salty waters mingled together, and new gods were born within them. Greatest among the first generation of gods were Anshar and his wife, Kishar. Then along came their first-born son, An, who was greater even than his father. In time An fathered Enki. And Enki surpassed all the other gods in strength and wisdom and understanding.

The younger gods were a noisy bunch, always laughing, quarreling, and playing games. Finally, Apsu could take no more of their clamor. He called for his vizier, Mummu. The two went and sat down before Tiamat. "The ways of our sons are disturbing me," Apsu complained. "I cannot rest by day. I cannot sleep by night. I have decided to destroy them, so that we may have peace and quiet."

When Tiamat heard her husband's words, she swelled up in anger. "What?" she exploded. "Would you destroy the lives that we ourselves created? Our offspring are troublesome indeed, but we must try to be patient."

Apsu might have heeded his wife, but Mummu leaned close to his ear. "Pay no attention to her, great father," whispered the counselor. "Those troublemakers show no respect for your authority. Destroy them, and you shall rest undisturbed again." That advice was just what Apsu had been hoping for. His face glowed with pleasure as he lifted up the vizier and embraced him. Then together the two made preparations for the destruction of the gods.

Word of their evil plot soon reached the younger gods. The rowdy group was stunned into silence. No one could see how to escape death at the hands of mighty Apsu—no one except Enki. While his brothers and sisters sat brooding, that wise god prepared an artful spell. He cast his magic over the deep waters, pouring sweet sleep upon Apsu. As the great god lay dozing, Enki took his crown and placed it upon his own head. He held Apsu down and slew him. Then Enki seized the dark counselor Mummu and cast him in a deep prison.

After subduing his enemies, Enki built a splendid chamber inside the still, sweet waters of Apsu. There he dwelled with his wife, Damkina. And there, in the heart of the holy waters, was born the god of gods, Marduk.

Marduk had a form so beautiful that no human mind can conceive it. He was taller, stronger, and bolder than any other god. He had four flashing eyes for limitless sight and four enormous ears for boundless hearing. When his lips moved, fire blazed from within him. Enki's spirit exulted when he beheld his newborn son, for he saw that Marduk was perfect.

An, the proud grandfather, created the four winds as a plaything for his magnificent grandson. In Marduk's hands the tempests blew from the north, south, east, and west, stirring up Tiamat's waters. Some of the older gods were annoyed by the storms. They took their complaints to Tiamat. "These frightful winds disturb your body, and we can find no rest," they grumbled. "You lay still and silent when Apsu was slain and Mummu was imprisoned. It is time to take revenge! Punish these tormentors who bring nothing but trouble for the ones who created them!"

Tiamat created eleven monsters, including the Great Lion.

Their angry words aroused Tiamat. Remembering her lost husband and his faithful counselor, she convened a council of war. Then the wrathful goddess set to work creating an army of monsters to march with her into battle. She made giant serpents with deadly fangs and poison for blood. She made roaring dragons clothed in terror and crowned with fiery halos. Eleven monsters in all she created, each one so fearsome that whoever beheld it would collapse in utter terror. Tiamat armed her demons with merciless weapons. She named her lover Kingu commander of her battle forces. Placing the sacred Tablet of Destinies on Kingu's breast, she proclaimed him supreme ruler of the universe.

News of Tiamat's evil plans soon reached Anshar. He called for a champion to oppose the goddess's army of gods and monsters. First Enki went forth to do battle. But when the god saw Tiamat's forces, he was stricken with terror and returned in shame to his grandfather. Next Anshar called for An. That hero strode forth. But when An beheld Tiamat's savage face, he too fled before her.

The demons in Tiamat's army struck terror in the hearts of the gods.

Anshar shook his head in despair. "Are we doomed?" asked the father of gods. "Is there no one who can face Tiamat?"

At that moment Marduk stepped forward. "Rejoice and be glad!" said the valiant god. "You shall soon set your foot upon the neck of Tiamat. But if I am to be your champion and destroy your enemies, you must make *me* king of the gods."

Anshar's heart swelled with joy at the young god's brave pronouncement. He summoned the gods to an assembly. They erected a splendid throne for Marduk and gave him the shining robes and scepter of a king. "We hereby grant you sovereignty over the entire universe," cried the great gods. "From this day onward, your word shall be law and your command everlasting."

Then Marduk armed himself for battle. He constructed a great bow and hung it at his side. He made a giant net to ensnare Tiamat. Grasping his mighty stone club, he mounted his terrible storm chariot. Lightning blazed before him and winds raged all around him as he set forth to meet Tiamat.

Kingu and his army saw the mighty hero approaching. Their eyes blurred at his magnificence, and they shrank back in confusion. Spitting savage defiance, Tiamat strode forward alone. The raging goddess flung

FACE TO FACE THEY CAME, TIAMAT AND MARDUK. . . .
THEY ENGAGED IN COMBAT, THEY CLOSED FOR BATTLE.

Enuma Elish

herself at Marduk. He quickly shot his net and entangled her. When Tiamat opened her jaws wide to consume him, he drove a fierce wind into her mouth, so that she could not close it. His other winds charged into Tiamat's body, swelling her belly. Then Marduk shot a single arrow. It tore through Tiamat's swollen belly, pierced her heart, and killed her.

After Tiamat had fallen, the gods who had followed her wept and trembled. Marduk smashed their weapons and took them captive. He trampled the eleven monsters underfoot, destroying their powers. He bound Kingu and stripped him of all authority. Then the noble god took the Tablet of Destinies that had been wrongly bestowed on Kingu and placed it on his own breast.

Returning to Tiamat, Marduk cut her huge body in two like a shell-fish. One half he raised up to form the sky. With the other half he made the foundation of the earth. He poked out her eyes and set them on the earth, so that the Tigris and Euphrates rivers could flow from them. Other parts of her body he fashioned into the streams, clouds, and mountains.

Next the great Marduk created the sun, moon, and stars. He determined the length of day and night, the phases of the moon, and the order of the seasons. He made An ruler of the heavens, Enlil the earth, and Enki the life-giving waters. He assigned realms to all the other gods, each to his place, so that they might work together harmoniously in the orderly world he had created.

When Marduk's work was finished, all the gods came together to worship him. Then they built a sanctuary to serve as their earthly home forever. Marduk named this glorious city Babylon, or "houses of the great gods."

But who would serve the gods' needs so they might live at ease in their new home? Once again Marduk had the answer. "We will put together bones and blood," he said. "We will create a new creature and call him man."

So Enki cut off the head of Kingu, who had led the rebellion. From the slain god's bones and blood, he fashioned the first human beings. Enki explained to the new creatures that the purpose of their lives was to serve the gods. Scribes wrote down his sacred instructions, so that the people would never forget them. And so it is that each year, men gather in the shrine of Marduk in Babylon. There they sing the praises of the god of gods, who defeated Tiamat and attained everlasting kingship.

THE ORIGINS *of* HUMANITY

The Rebellion of the Gods

IN *ENUMA ELISH*, THE BABYLONIAN POEM THAT WAS THE source for our first myth, the creation of human beings was almost an afterthought. Marduk defeated his enemies, created the world, and assigned realms to all the gods. Only after those important tasks were completed did he order Enki to produce human beings.

In *Atrahasis*, the source for the myth that follows here, human creation is a much more important part of the tale. *Atrahasis*, a Babylonian poem composed sometime around the nineteenth century BCE, starts out with the story of human creation. It then takes listeners through a long mythological history of the early human race.

According to *Atrahasis*, the early world was no paradise. A host of minor gods were stuck with the backbreaking job of digging and maintaining the canals. After years of labor, the gods refused to work any longer. Enki came up with a solution to the crisis. With the help of the birth goddess Nintu, the wise god created men and women to take over the burden of labor.

Opposite: Mesopotamian myths tell us that the gods created humans to relieve themselves of life's tiresome tasks.

Like the mortals in *Enuma Elish*, the people created in *Atrahasis* have only one purpose in life: to free the gods from hard labor. Yet the men and women in this Babylonian tale are not portrayed simply as lowly creatures. Enki and Nintu make the first people by combining clay with the spit, blood, and flesh of the gods. That formula tells us that humans are complex beings containing elements of both the earthly and divine worlds.

CAST *of* CHARACTERS

An (ahn) God of the heavens
Enlil (EN-lil) God of the earth
Enki (EN-kee) God of the waters and wisdom
Nusku (NUS-koo) Enlil's vizier, or chief adviser
Nintu (NIN-too) Goddess of birth

IN THE BEGINNING the great gods cast lots to divide up the world. An, father of the gods, got the heavenly realm above the earth. His son Enlil would rule the earth itself. The command of the fresh waters that are the source of all rivers and streams went to another son of An, Enki the wise.

After An went up to the heavens, Enlil put the lesser gods to work digging out the canals that form the lifelines of the earth. Day and night the young gods labored over their picks and shovels. They dug out deep channels and worked to keep them clear. They even dug out the beds of the Tigris and Euphrates rivers.

After many years of labor, the weary gods began to groan and grumble. Finally, one of them threw down his shovel. "Come! Let us confront Enlil and make him relieve us of all this work and trouble," he shouted. "Now, my brothers! To war! To battle!"

As the other gods heard this speech, their tempers flared. With a roar they tossed their shovels in a great pile and set fire to them. Then they snatched up blazing torches and set out for the shrine where Enlil dwelt in ease and comfort.

It was the middle of the night when the angry mob reached Enlil's dwelling. The god lay sleeping, but his vizier Nusku heard the clamor. Rousing his master, Nusku cried, "My lord, your house is surrounded! A rabble has come, bringing battle to your very gate!"

Enlil jumped out of bed. He sprang for his weapons. "Lock the gate, Nusku," he commanded. "Take your weapon and stand before me."

Nusku took his position, holding his weapon at the ready. "Great lord, your face is as pale as the tamarisk," he said to his master. "These gods are like your own children. Why are you afraid of them? Send for An and Enki, and together hold a council to determine how to deal with the rebels."

So Enlil sent out his messengers. An came down from the heavens, and Enki rose from the waters. "A rabble has come to my door!" Enlil told them. "Why have they risen against me? Shall I wage battle?"

"Let Nusku go and find out who is in charge of the uprising," An answered calmly.

Nusku went out and spoke with the rebels. Returning, he delivered their answer: "Every single one of us has declared war! Every single one of us has risen against Enlil! Our work is too hard, our burden too great. Our excessive labors are killing us!"

When Enlil heard this message, he nearly wept with fear and anger. But Enki saw the situation more clearly. "We cannot blame the rebels," said the wise god. "Their work *was* too hard. Their burden *was* too great. Every day the earth has resounded with the sounds of their labor, and we have ignored the warning signals. Now let Nintu create mortals to take over the gods' workload."

So Nintu the birth goddess was brought before the council. Enki issued his instructions, and together the two began the complex process of creation. Enki prepared a sacred bath. The great gods purified themselves at the new moon, the seventh day, and the full moon. Then they chose one of the rebels and sacrificed him for the good of his brothers.

Nintu took clay and mixed it with the flesh and blood of the slain god, in order to give humans an immortal spirit. The great gods moistened the mixture with their divine spittle. As Nintu chanted her magical incantations, Enki worked the clay the way a man kneads mud for bricks. When it was ready, Nintu pinched off fourteen pieces. Fourteen young goddesses shaped the pieces of clay into statues, seven male and seven female. Nintu placed the statues in a special chamber.

> [NINTU] PINCHED OFF FOURTEEN PIECES OF CLAY, AND SET SEVEN PIECES ON THE RIGHT, SEVEN ON THE LEFT.
> ⌐ ATRAHASIS

Nine months later, Nintu returned to the birthing chamber. Just as a midwife helps a pregnant woman give birth, she opened the chamber. She brought forth the humans, seven men and seven women.

Nintu instructed the creatures in the proper ways to celebrate marriage and childbirth, so that the human race might flourish. Then the men made picks and shovels. With their new tools, the humans took over the backbreaking labor that feeds the people and sustains the gods who created them.

THE MESOPOTAMIANS SPEAK
ENKI BLESSES *the* WORLD

Like the Babylonians, the Sumerians honored Enki as their creator and greatest champion. An ancient Sumerian poem known as "Enki and the World Order" explains how the wise god blessed the earth with prosperity and abundance. Not surprisingly, the poem shows Enki lavishing his finest gifts on Sumer. In the following passage, the god is praising his own works of creation.

> I am the lord, I am one whose command is unquestioned, I am the foremost
> in all things,
> At my command the stalls have been built, the sheepfolds have been enclosed,
> When I approached heaven a rain of prosperity poured down from heaven,
> When I approached the earth, there was a high flood,
> When I approached its green meadows,
> The heaps and mounds were [piled] up at my word. . . .
>
> O Sumer, great land, of the lands of the universe,
> Filled with steadfast brightness, the people from sunrise to sunset obedient to
> the divine decrees,
> Thy decrees are exalted decrees, unreachable,
> Thy heart is profound, unfathomable. . . .
> The . . . great gods,
> In thy midst have taken up their dwelling place,
> In thy large groves they consume [their] food.
>
> O house of Sumer, may thy stables be many, may thy cows multiply,
> May thy sheepfolds be many, may thy sheep be myriad [numerous].

Above: A peaceful milking scene illustrates the prosperity of Sumer.

THE WRATH
of the GODS

The Great Flood

OUR NEXT MYTH CONTINUES THE STORY OF THE EARLY human race as told in *Atrahasis.* Hundreds of years after the creation of the first men and women, the world has become overpopulated and very noisy. Enlil decides to wipe out the troublesome humans with a massive flood. Enki objects to his brother's harsh scheme. He warns his favorite mortal, King Atrahasis ("extra wise"). The king builds a boat and rides out the flood, saving humankind from destruction.

Stories of a great flood were told by ancient peoples in nearly every region of the world. *Atrahasis*, written in Babylonian times, is the oldest known of these myths. A later version of the Mesopotamian flood story is found in *The Epic of Gilgamesh.* (See page 75 for a retelling of that great adventure tale.) Many scholars believe that these Mesopotamian tales may have inspired the most famous flood story of all: the ancient Hebrews' account of Noah and the ark.

The Mesopotamian flood story celebrates the power of the gods

Opposite:
Atrahasis rode out the great flood in his boat, saving humankind from destruction.

and Enki's role as humankind's greatest champion. It also reflects the complex relationship between the human and divine worlds. According to mythology, the people of Mesopotamia depended on the gods for their creation and survival. After the great flood, the gods realized that in turn they were dependent on humans, whose hard work and offerings made the divine way of life possible.

CAST *of* CHARACTERS

Enlil (EN-lil) God of the earth
Atrahasis (ah-trah-HAH-sis) Mythological Babylonian king; also known as Utnapishtim
Enki (EN-kee) God of the waters and wisdom
Namtar (NAHM-tar) God of disease, pestilence, and death
Adad (AH-dahd) God of the rain and storms
Nintu (NIN-too) Goddess of birth

TWELVE HUNDRED YEARS had passed since the creation. Twelve hundred years, and the world had become a crowded and noisy place. Enlil, who rules over the earth, could hardly bear the clamor. "The noise of humankind is like a bellowing bull," he complained to the other gods. "I am losing sleep because of their never-ending racket! Let us send disease to reduce the earth's troublesome population."

So the great gods sent a dreadful plague. Many men, women, and children sickened and died. Atrahasis, a wise and reverent king, opened his heart to his personal god, Enki. "How long, O Lord, will the gods make us suffer?" asked the king. "Will you not put an end to this pestilence?"

When Enki heard the good king, his heart was moved to pity. "Send heralds throughout the land," he told Atrahasis. "The people shall not send their prayers and offerings to any god but Namtar, bringer of disease and pestilence. When the offerings reach Namtar, he may remove his dark hand from the earth."

Atrahasis followed his god's instructions. He sent out the heralds, and the people offered their freshly baked loaves to Namtar. When the god received all the fragrant offerings, he was pleased. He withdrew his hand, and disease left the earth.

Adad held power over both destructive storms and life-giving rains.

Another twelve hundred years passed. Again the earth overflowed with people. "These noisy humans are more numerous than before!" complained Enlil. "Let Adad withhold the rains. Let the rivers run dry and the crops fail, so that these troublesome mortals perish from hunger."

So the great gods sent a terrible drought. The rains stopped, and the floodwaters ceased to rise from the rivers. Crops withered in the dry earth. Many men, women, and children died of starvation. Once again Atrahasis spoke with his god, Enki. "How long, O Lord, will hunger consume the country?" he asked. "Will you not put an end to our suffering?"

Again Enki answered his faithful servant: "Let your heralds make a loud noise throughout the land. The people shall not send their prayers and offerings to any god but Adad, bringer of rain. When the offerings reach Adad, he may remove his dark hand from the earth."

So the people offered their fragrant loaves to Adad. When their gifts reached the god, he made mist form in the morning and dewdrops in the evening. The earth was renewed, and the fields delivered crops in abundance.

Enki ended the terrible famine by causing masses of fish to fall into the waters.

Another twelve hundred years passed. Again the earth became too crowded, and again Enlil called for the destruction of the unruly people. He placed a guard on all of nature's bounty, so that no means of nourishment could reach the human race. Many men, women, and children suffered and died in the dreadful famine. But once more Atrahasis appealed to Enki. This time the merciful god let large quantities of fish fall into the waters to feed the starving people.

Now Enlil was furious. "I am losing sleep because of Enki's meddling!" the god shouted. "He is responsible for this problem, and he can fix it! Enki must wipe out the noisy creatures he created."

All the great gods were distressed by the quarrel between the divine brothers. Human beings were not worth the trouble they were causing! So the gods decreed that Enki must use his powers to create a flood and wipe out the human race. And to make sure nothing interfered with their plans this time, they made the meddlesome god swear an oath not to speak to the humans.

But Enki was clever. He quickly thought up a way to warn Atrahasis without violating the oath he had taken. That night the king was sitting outside a house of reeds near the river. A gentle wind sprang up. Listening carefully, Atrahasis thought that he heard the breeze speaking, not to him but to the wall of the house. "Reed hut, pay close attention!" it seemed to whisper. "Forsake your home and possessions, and seek life! Build a giant boat with many decks and a strong roof for shelter. Fill the boat with the seed of all living things. In seven days' time, a great flood shall befall you."

The next morning Atrahasis began to build his boat. The entire community helped him. Rich and poor, old and young worked together to construct the enormous hull. They sewed the planks together with cords. They sealed the cracks with tar. After six days the work was completed. The king loaded the boat with birds, cattle, and every other type of animal. He invited his family on board for a feast. He also brought aboard skilled craftspeople to keep alive the knowledge of arts and crafts.

On the morning of the seventh day, the face of the weather changed. A cloud as black as night rose above the horizon. The winds began to rage, and the rains began to fall. Atrahasis cut through the rope that held the boat to the land. Then he went inside and sealed the door behind him.

Swiftly the storm gods unleashed by Enki tore across the earth. They bellowed from the clouds. They raked the sky with lightning. They poured down rain, smashing homes and shrines like tiny clay pots. The people of the earth were swept away in the deluge, and the huge boat was tossed about on the waters.

THE FLOOD ROARED LIKE A BULL, LIKE A WILD ASS SCREAMING THE WINDS HOWLED.
— ATRAHASIS

Even the gods became frightened of the storm's fury. Wailing at the world's destruction, they scrambled up to the highest heavens. There they cowered like dogs. Their mouths grew parched, and their bellies felt empty. There were no humans left to offer gifts and satisfy their hunger.

For seven days and seven nights, the downpour continued. Then, on the dawn of the eighth day, the storm left off its battle. The winds stilled. The rains ceased. The sea all around became as flat as a mirror.

The boat came to rest on the tip of a mountain submerged in the sea. Atrahasis opened the door and peered out over the calm waters.

AFTER *the* FLOOD

After the rains ended, Atrahasis released a series of birds. When the third bird failed to return, he knew that it had found dry land. The king left his boat and made a sacrifice, burning fragrant plants and branches to attract the gods to his offering. The following passage is the way Atrahasis told the flood story in *The Epic of Gilgamesh* (see page 75).

When the seventh day arrived,
I brought out a dove and set it free.
The dove went off and returned,
No landing place came to its view, so it turned back.
I brought out a swallow and set it free,
The swallow went off and returned,
No landing place came to its view, so it turned back.
I brought out a raven and set it free,
The raven went off and saw the ebbing of the waters.
It ate, preened, left droppings, did not turn back. . . .
I brought out an offering and offered it to the four directions.
I set up an incense offering on the summit of the mountain,
I arranged seven and seven cult vessels,
I heaped reeds, cedar, and myrtle in their bowls.
The gods smelled the savor,
The gods smelled the sweet savor,
The gods crowded round the sacrificer like flies.

Above: A priest presents his prayers and offerings to the gods.

Everywhere was a solemn silence, for nearly all of humankind had perished. The good king fell to his knees and wept at the devastation.

After a while Atrahasis set loose a bird. It soared over the vast expanse of the sea, then came back to the ship. The king sent out a second bird, but it too returned. Finally, he released a glossy black raven. When the raven failed to return, Atrahasis knew that it had found dry land.

In time the waters receded. Atrahasis sent forth his passengers, human and animal. Then the king sent up a burnt offering to give thanks for his salvation. When the sweet odor of the sacrifice reached the heavens, all the gods and goddesses were overjoyed. All except Enlil. "We swore an oath," the enraged god protested. "No form of life was supposed to escape destruction! Who is responsible for this act of defiance?"

"I did it," answered Enki. "O Enlil, you are great in wisdom. Punish the sinner for his sin and the criminal for his crime. But let us be merciful, so that humankind is not cut off completely, leaving us starving for their sacrifices."

The god's well-chosen words soothed his brother. Summoning the birth goddess Nintu, Enlil issued a new proclamation: "Henceforth let some mortal women be barren. Let some lose their newborn infants. In addition let there be priestesses who devote their lives to the temples and never bear children. In this way we shall reduce the earth's future population and spare the human race."

As the god spoke, a rainbow appeared in the heavens, as a sign of his promise that the great flood would never return to wipe out humanity. Enlil took Atrahasis and his wife by the hand. He touched their foreheads and blessed them. "Until now you were mortal," he proclaimed. "Now you shall be like the gods and live forever." And with these words, Enlil led the king and queen to a new dwelling in a distant land at the source of the rivers.

A LOST CHANCE *for* IMMORTALITY

Adapa and the South Wind

ACCORDING TO MESOPOTAMIAN MYTHOLOGY, THE GODS gave all the arts of civilization to humankind. They often bestowed these gifts through wise men, or sages. The gods instructed the sages in government, scholarship, religious rituals, arts, crafts, and other aspects of civilized behavior. These special mortals then shared their superior knowledge with the rest of the human race.

The first of the sages was Adapa, chief priest of Enki in the city of Eridu. Enki gave his beloved priest every quality of the gods except one: immortality. In "Adapa and the South Wind," we learn that the sage has accidentally angered An, god of the heavens. When An calls Adapa before him for judgment, Enki tells the mortal how to soften the great god's wrath. Enki also gives Adapa some deceitful advice. He tells the man not to accept An's offers of food and drink—gifts that would have made him immortal.

Opposite:
A sage, or wise man, poses in reverent silence before the gods.

The myth of Adapa has been pieced together from fragments of clay tablets discovered in King Assurbanipal's library at Nineveh and at other sites. Scholars disagree over the meaning of this ancient tale. Does Enki deceive Adapa because he does not want his servant to become a god like himself? Is he trying to help mortals by making sure the sage remains among them? Perhaps Adapa is being punished for rejecting An's hospitality. Perhaps he is not wise enough to disobey his master's instructions. Or is the myth simply telling us that no human (except the legendary Atrahasis) is meant to live forever? The people of ancient Mesopotamia would have known the answer to these questions. Today we can only enjoy the story and draw our own conclusions.

CAST *of* CHARACTERS

Adapa (AH-dah-pah) Mythical priest and sage
Enki (EN-kee) God of the waters and wisdom
An (ahn) God of the heavens
Dumuzi (doo-MOO-zih) God of vegetation and fertility
Gizzida (GIZ-ih-dah) Gatekeeper of heaven

I N THE CITY OF ERIDU lived a sage named Adapa. Enki had created Adapa when the world was new to serve as a protecting spirit among humankind. He gave the sage all the knowledge, wisdom, and power of the gods. He made Adapa pure and holy, so the man could serve as chief priest in the temple where Enki made his earthly home. One blessing only had the god denied his chosen servant. That was the gift of eternal life.

Each day Adapa performed the sacred rites in Enki's temple. He set up the offering table before the god's holy image. He heaped the table with fragrant loaves of bread and other food. The priest baked the bread with his own pure hands. He sailed out in his own little boat to catch the fish that were so pleasing to the god of the waters.

One day Adapa was drifting upon the waters, waiting for the fish to fill his nets. Suddenly the South Wind spotted the sailboat. With a gleeful laugh, it began to beat its giant wings. The waters rippled. They churned. They rose up in giant waves. Adapa held on for his life as the little boat tossed about like a leaf upon the raging sea. Then came one mighty gust. The boat overturned, and the priest plunged into the water. As he struggled among the waves, he raised his fist and spluttered, "South Wind, for this I will break your wing!"

The South Wind beat its wings, overturning Adapa's boat.

No sooner had Adapa uttered his curse than the wing was broken. With a wail the South Wind limped off toward the horizon, and the sea grew calm. Climbing back into his boat, the priest said a prayer of thanksgiving. Then he went on with his fishing.

For the next seven days, the South Wind did not blow. Up in the heavens, An noticed the still waters. The god sent a messenger to find out what had happened. When the servant returned with news of the wind's broken wing, An was furious. Rising up on his exalted throne, the great god cried, "Bring that mortal to me!"

Enki knew of An's command, for he sees and hears all that happens in heaven and earth. Fearing for his favorite mortal, the wise god gave Adapa careful instructions: "You will be summoned before the judgment throne of An, king of the heavens. You must unbind your hair and put on your mourning clothes. When you approach the Gate of An, you will see the two divine gatekeepers, Dumuzi and Gizzida. They will ask why you are dressed like a man in mourning. You must tell them that you grieve for two gods who have vanished from your country."

Adapa did as he was instructed. When An's messenger arrived in Eridu, he found the priest dressed in a ragged mourning robe. Adapa was taken up to heaven. There he saw Dumuzi and Gizzida standing guard before the Gate of An.

"Young man, why are you dressed like that?" the gatekeepers asked.

"Two great gods have vanished from the earth," said Adapa. "I am mourning their absence."

"Who are these two gods that have vanished?" asked the guards.

"Dumuzi and Gizzida," the priest answered.

Just as Enki had expected, the two guards looked at each other and laughed. They were pleased and flattered by the man's devotion. Regarding Adapa with friendly eyes, they ushered the priest into An's presence.

But the great An was in no mood for laughter. The moment he saw Adapa, he shouted, "Come here! Why did you meddle with the South Wind?"

"Great lord," replied the priest, "I was out catching fish for the house of my master, Enki. The South Wind blew and sank my boat. In my fury I broke its wing."

An hesitated, impressed by Adapa's modest and respectful manner.

Then Dumuzi and Gizzida spoke up in the priest's favor. They said that Adapa was a righteous young man who was devoted to the gods. They pleaded with their master to spare the good mortal from punishment.

At their words, An's anger faded. He looked on the priest with new-found sympathy. "Why did Enki disclose the ways of heaven and earth to a mere mortal?" the great god muttered to himself. "So much wisdom and knowledge without immortality can only bring unhappiness." Then, with a smile, An called for his servants. "Come! Bring oil and a new garment for Adapa. Fetch the bread of eternal life, and let him eat it! Fetch the water of eternal life, and let him drink it!"

An's servants fetched a fine new garment, and Adapa put it on. They brought oil, and the priest anointed himself with it. But when they offered Adapa bread and water, he would not touch them. The faithful priest had remembered a warning that far-seeing Enki had given him: "When you stand before An, he will offer you food and drink.

> THEY FETCHED HIM THE BREAD OF LIFE, BUT HE WOULD NOT EAT. THEY FETCHED HIM THE WATER OF LIFE, BUT HE WOULD NOT DRINK.
> ⁓ "ADAPA AND THE SOUTH WIND"

Do not eat the bread, for it is the bread of death. Do not drink the water, for it is the water of death."

An laughed as the young man refused his precious gifts. "Come now, Adapa!" he said. "Why don't you eat? Why don't you drink? Don't you want to live forever? Alas, despite all your powers, you are still a foolish mortal."

Then An told his servants to take Adapa back to earth. There would be no second chance at immortality. To this very day, men and women may achieve wisdom but eternal life belongs to the gods only.

INANNA TAKES
the ME

The Sumerians believed that Enki gave the arts of civilization to humankind in the form of *me*. The *me* were the divine laws that formed the foundation of social institutions, religious practices, human conditions, and other aspects of society. There were more than one hundred of these marvelous decrees, including kingship, the priesthood, art, music, truth, wisdom, and crafts such as woodworking and basket weaving.

According to mythology, Enki kept the *me* in his deep-sea shrine at Eridu. The goddess Inanna wanted them for her own city, Uruk (also known as Erech). Inanna traveled to Eridu in her heavenly boat. She persuaded Enki to hand over the divine decrees. When the god realized what he had done, he sent his messenger Isimud with an army of sea monsters after Inanna. A poem inscribed on a four-thousand-year-old clay tablet from Nippur describes what happened when Isimud caught up with the goddess.

Above: Inanna was the patron goddess of the Sumerian city-state of Uruk.

"Oh Inanna [said Isimud], thy [heavenly] father has sent me to thee,
Thy father, exalted in his speech,
Enki, exalted in his utterance,
His great words are not to go unheeded."

Holy Inanna answers him:
"My father, what has he spoken to thee, what has he said to thee?
His great words that are not to go unheeded, what pray are they?"

"My king has spoken to me,
Enki has said to me:
'Let Inanna go to Erech,
But thou, bring me back the boat of heaven to Eridu.'"

Holy Inanna said to the messenger Isimud:
"My father, why pray has he changed his word to me,
Why has he broken his righteous word to me,
Why has he defiled his great words to me?
My father has spoken to me falsehood, has spoken to me falsehood,
Falsely has he uttered the name of his power. . . ."

Barely had she uttered these words,
The sea monsters seized the boat of heaven.

THE CYCLE *of the* SEASONS

Inanna Descends to the Underworld

INANNA WAS ANCIENT MESOPOTAMIA'S MOST POPULAR deity. As queen of heaven and earth, she watched over love, fertility, and war. This powerful goddess was capable of passionate devotion. She could also be temperamental, violent, and cruel.

In "Inanna Descends to the Underworld," the goddess shows her many different faces. During a journey to the Land of No Return, she is taken prisoner by her sister, Ereshkigal, queen of that dark and gloomy realm. Enki finds a way to set Inanna free. However, not even a goddess may leave the land of the dead without providing a substitute to take her place. In a fit of temper, Inanna chooses her beloved husband, Dumuzi (the god we met in "Adapa and the South Wind," in his sometime role as gatekeeper of heaven). Dumuzi is saved from eternal imprisonment only after his faithful sister Geshtinanna agrees to take his place in the underworld for six months each year.

Opposite:
A modern-day painting shows the gentle side of Inanna, beloved goddess of love and fertility.

To the ancient Mesopotamians, the story of Inanna and Dumuzi explained the annual cycle of the seasons. When Dumuzi dwelled in the land of the dead, the earth entered a period of infertility. His return to Inanna brought new life each spring.

Inanna's descent also may have had a deeper meaning. In the myth the goddess gives up her earthly power and glory to surrender to her "dark side," represented by her gloomy sister Ereshkigal. Through this spiritual journey, Inanna is reborn. When she returns to earth, she brings her newfound knowledge of the eternal life of the spirit to humankind.

CAST of CHARACTERS

Inanna (ih-NAH-nah) Goddess of love, fertility, and war
Dumuzi (doo-MOO-zih) God of vegetation and fertility
Ninshubur (NIN-shuh-ber) Friend and servant of Inanna
Enki (EN-kee) God of the waters and wisdom
Petuh (PAY-tuh) Gatekeeper of the underworld
Ereshkigal (er-esh-KIG-uhl) Queen of the underworld
Asushunamir (ah-SOO-shuh-nah-mer) Spirit-guide who
    rescues Inanna
Geshtinanna (gesh-tin-AN-ah) Dumuzi's sister

INANNA, QUEEN OF HEAVEN AND EARTH, had searched the world for a husband. At last she had found the love of her life, the shepherd Dumuzi. Together the two lovers had wandered in spring gardens. In their bliss they had eyes only for each other. But after they were married, Dumuzi changed. He became withdrawn, always busy tending to his new duties as king of all Sumer. Inanna was left lonely and unsatisfied. One day she heard a distant wailing from far below. Suddenly, deep in her heart, she felt a longing to journey down to the dark and mysterious Land of No Return.

In preparation for her journey, Inanna gathered the seven sacred symbols of her earthly power about her. First, she put on her queenly robes. Then she placed her great crown on her head. She put sparkling rings in her ears and tied lapis lazuli beads around her neck. She bound a golden breastplate about her breast and a jeweled girdle around her waist. Lastly she slipped golden bands over her wrists and ankles.

Adorned with these divine protections, Inanna called for her faithful friend and servant, the goddess Ninshubur. "I am descending to the underworld," said Inanna. "If in three days I have not returned, fill heaven and earth with lamentations for me. Go to the house of Enki and cry, 'Do not let your daughter Inanna be lost forever!' Enki, lord of wisdom, keeps the bread and water of life. Surely he will not let me die in the underworld."

Then Inanna descended to the land where the spirits dwell in darkness,

> INANNA ABANDONED HEAVEN,
> ABANDONED EARTH,
> TO THE NETHER WORLD
> SHE DESCENDED.
> — "INANNA DESCENDS TO THE UNDERWORLD"

with clay for bread and dust for water. She reached the outer gate of that gloomy kingdom. There she cried in a proud and haughty voice, "Open up! Let me in, or I shall smash the door!"

"Who are you?" asked Petuh, gatekeeper of the underworld.

"I am Inanna, queen of heaven and earth," replied the goddess. "I have come to see my older sister, Ereshkigal."

Petuh asked the goddess to wait. He went to the palace of Ereshkigal, queen of the underworld. "Your sister waits outside the palace gates," he told the dark queen. "She is wearing the radiant ornaments of her earthly power."

Ereshkigal struck her thigh in anger. "Why does my sister bring her light and glory to a land where all is darkness and misery?" she raged. "Go, Petuh. Open the seven gates of the underworld to Inanna. But treat her according to the ancient rules, so that the queen of heaven may enter bowed low."

So Petuh opened the outer gate of the underworld. As Inanna entered, he removed her crown. "Why do you take the great crown from my head?" asked the goddess.

"Enter, my lady. Thus are the rules of the underworld," said the gatekeeper.

Inanna passed through the second gate. Petuh took the sparkling rings from her ears. "Why do you remove my earrings?" asked the goddess.

"Thus are the rules of the underworld," replied the gatekeeper.

Inanna passed through the third, fourth, fifth, and sixth gates. Each time the gatekeeper stripped away one of her ornaments. He took her lapis lazuli beads, her golden breastplate, and her jeweled girdle. He took the golden bands from her wrists and ankles. Finally, Inanna entered the seventh gate, and Petuh took the queenly robes from her body.

Stripped of her earthly powers, Inanna was brought before the throne. She was forced to bow low before her sister. "How dare you

Ereshkigal, queen of the underworld, unleashed her evil forces against Inanna.

enter my realm!" shrieked Ereshkigal. "Sixty curses I pronounce upon you!" Instantly sixty diseases afflicted every part of Inanna's body. The stricken goddess was turned into a corpse. The dark queen ordered her servants to hang her sister's body from a hook on the wall of the palace.

For three days and nights, Inanna remained a captive. On the fourth day, Ninshubur dressed in mourning. With tears flowing down her face, the faithful servant went to Enki and told him that Inanna was imprisoned in the Land of No Return.

Enki was troubled at the loss of the bright goddess. For a moment he pondered the problem. Then, in his wisdom, the great god created Asushunamir, a being of light who was neither male nor female. Enki gave the beautiful creature skin bags holding the bread and water of life. Then he sent his creation on a mission to the underworld.

Like light itself, Enki's wondrous creation slipped through the seven gates. Asushunamir entered the throne room, where the dark queen sat nursing her bitterness. When Ereshkigal moaned, Asushunamir moaned. When Ereshkigal sighed, the creature echoed her sighing. Gradually the queen felt her loneliness easing. She looked up and beheld the beautiful, sympathetic being.

"You have lightened my mood, good spirit," said Ereshkigal. "What can I give you in return? I swear by the great gods, whatever you name, you shall have it."

"I want only the meat hanging on the wall," answered Asushunamir.

"That belongs to my sister, Inanna."

"I want the body of Inanna."

Hearing Asushunamir's demand, Ereshkigal knew that she had been tricked. But the dark queen had made a vow, and she must honor it. Eyes blazing with fury, she ordered her servants to take down Inanna's body. "Now go!" the queen shrieked. "Take my wretched sister, and get out of my kingdom!"

Asushunamir carried Inanna's lifeless body outside the palace. The creature placed the goddess on the ground and sprinkled her sixty times with the bread and water of life. The goddess stirred. She awoke. Then she rose and made her way to the gates of the underworld.

Through each of the gates Inanna passed. At each, Petuh gave back one of her shining ornaments. At last she stood before the final gate, as strong and radiant as ever. Petuh placed the great crown on her head. As she turned to leave, the gatekeeper spoke a warning: "No one may return to the world above without paying a ransom. You must send someone to take your place, or return and dwell here forever. Thus are the rules of the underworld."

Inanna stepped through the final gate, and a whole company of demons followed. The heartless demons who tear the wife from the husband's arms, who steal the child from the mother's lap and father's knee, swarmed all around her. Large demons marched before and behind her, bearing jagged axes. Small demons clung to her sides, whispering and cackling.

Outside the gate Ninshubur was waiting. When the faithful servant saw her mistress surrounded by the shades of the dead, she threw herself down in the dust at Inanna's feet. The demons clapped their hands gleefully. "We will take this being down to the lower regions in your place, O Inanna," they shouted.

"No!" said the goddess. "Ninshubur has been my constant friend and companion. Because of her, my life was saved. I will find another."

So Inanna ascended to the earth. She walked through Sumer, accompanied by the ghastly crowd of demons. Everywhere she went, she saw her loyal subjects grieving for her absence. In each city the demons threatened to seize a victim to take Inanna's place in the underworld. Each time the goddess restrained them.

Finally, Inanna arrived in her own city, Uruk. She entered the palace and saw Dumuzi. Her husband was dressed not in mourning but in the magnificent robes that she herself had given him. Instead of weeping for his lost wife, he was seated on his high throne, tending to business as if she had never left him. The king looked

THE LARGE [DEMONS] WERE LIKE REEDS THE SIZE OF HIGH PICKET FENCES.
⌐ "INANNA DESCENDS TO THE UNDERWORLD"

A sharp-toothed demon of the underworld

down and beheld Inanna. He grimaced at the sight of the nasty demons. Then he returned to the important tasks of government.

Inanna quivered with rage. Raising a trembling hand, she pointed at her husband. "Take him!" she cried. "Take Dumuzi to the underworld!"

The demons howled in triumph. They grabbed Dumuzi, hauled him from the throne, and hacked him with their axes. Then they dragged the wailing king down to the underworld.

Thus Inanna reclaimed her high throne. But after a while, she began to regret her rash decision. She had lost the love of her youth forever. With him had gone all of life's sweetness. Consumed with a mixture of grief and wounded pride, the goddess wept bitter tears. As she wept, all of Sumer joined in her sorrow. No plants blossomed in the fields. No lambs were born in the sheepfold, no calves in the meadows. There was no love between man and woman, and no newborn children.

One day the grieving queen was wandering about the streets of Uruk when she came upon Dumuzi's sister, Geshtinanna. The devoted maiden was searching for her brother. Her clothes were torn and covered with dust, her cheeks streaked with tears. Her sorrow melted Inanna's proud heart. The goddess took her earthly sister by the hand. "Dumuzi is no more," she said gently. "He has been taken to the underworld by the demons."

"I want to comfort him. I want to share his fate," cried Geshtinanna. "The day will not dawn for me until it dawns for my brother."

Moved by the loving sister's devotion, Inanna resolved to grant her wish. Together the goddess and the mortal woman journeyed to the edge of the underworld. There they found Dumuzi waiting. "Henceforth you will go to the underworld for half of each year," Inanna told her husband. "Your sister will go for the other half. On the day Geshtinanna takes your place, that day you will return to me."

So it is that Inanna and her husband are separated for half a year, and the earth is plunged in mourning. Then Geshtinanna takes her brother's place in the underworld, and Inanna and Dumuzi are reunited. In that joyous season, their love lights the heavens, the wheat ripens in the field, and the newborn lambs bleat in the sheepfold.

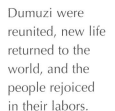

When Inanna and Dumuzi were reunited, new life returned to the world, and the people rejoiced in their labors.

THE MESOPOTAMIANS SPEAK
THE JOY *of* SUMER

The people of Mesopotamia celebrated the earth's awakening each spring with the Sacred Marriage ceremony. In this ancient ritual, the king played the role of Dumuzi and a high priestess or the queen took the part of Inanna. Through her union with the mortal king, the goddess descended to earth and united with the people. That ensured fertility and prosperity throughout the coming season. This hymn was composed around 1900 BCE to celebrate the Sacred Marriage of Inanna and a Sumerian king.

Above: A king reclines on a couch in his royal garden, enjoying a bowl of wine with his queen.

The people of Sumer assemble in the palace,
The house which guides the land.
The king builds a throne for the queen of the palace,
He sits beside her on the throne. . . .

The people cleanse the rushes with sweet-smelling cedar oil,
They arrange the rushes for the bed.
They spread a bridal sheet over the bed.
A bridal sheet to rejoice the heart, . . .
A bridal sheet for Inanna and Dumuzi. . . .

The king bids the people enter the great hall.
The people bring food offerings and bowls.
They burn juniper resin, perform laving [bathing] rites,
And pile up sweet-smelling incense.

The king embraces his beloved bride,
Dumuzi embraces Inanna.
Inanna, seated on the royal throne, shines like daylight.
The king, like the sun, shines radiantly by her side.
He arranges abundance, lushness, and plenty before her.
He assembles the people of Sumer. . . .

The people spend the day in plenty.
The king stands before the assembly in great joy.
He hails Inanna with the praises of the gods and the assembly:
"Holy Priestess! Created with the heavens and earth,
Inanna, First Daughter of the Moon, Lady of the Evening!
I sing your praises."

A HEROIC QUEST

The Epic of Gilgamesh

THE EPIC OF GILGAMESH IS THE WORLD'S OLDEST adventure story. Scholars believe that this ancient work of literature was inspired by a real-life king who ruled the Sumerian city-state of Uruk around 2700 BCE. Imaginative tales from the life of King Gilgamesh were first written down around 2100 BCE. Centuries later, Babylonian scribes collected these separate episodes and created one long narrative poem. Archaeologists have found versions of the Gilgamesh poem in several different languages in ancient sites across the Middle East. In modern times the story has been translated into more than a dozen languages and retold in novels, operas, and plays.

Our retelling of *The Epic of Gilgamesh* is based mainly on the "standard version," a seventh-century BCE text discovered in the ruins of King Assurbanipal's library at Nineveh. As this sweeping saga begins, the people of Uruk are suffering under their mighty but arrogant king. The gods decide to teach Gilgamesh a lesson by creating Enkidu, a

Opposite: The super-human king Gilgamesh vanquished ferocious lions and monsters.

wild man with strength and courage to match him. After a fierce battle, the two heroes become friends and set out on a quest for fame and glory. They face incredible perils and perform daring deeds. Then Enkidu dies. Brokenhearted and frightened at the idea of his own mortality, Gilgamesh begins a second quest, this time alone, to find the secret of eternal life. His adventures lead him to Atrahasis, the legendary king who was granted immortality after the great flood.

One of the reasons for the timeless appeal of *The Epic of Gilgamesh* is its universal themes. This ancient tale speaks of friendship, courage, hope, despair, the fear of death, and the longing for eternal life—themes as fresh and powerful today as they were four thousand years ago. In the end Gilgamesh learns that the only form of immortality humans can achieve is the lasting fame earned through great deeds. He also discovers that life is a precious gift that is meant to be enjoyed to the fullest.

CAST *of* CHARACTERS

Gilgamesh (GIL-gah-mesh) Legendary king of Uruk
Ninsun (NIN-sun) Divine mother of Gilgamesh
Lugalbanda (loo-gal-BAN-dah) Mortal father of
    Gilgamesh
Inanna (ih-NAH-nah) Goddess of love, fertility, and war
An (ahn) God of the heavens
Nintu (NIN-too) Goddess of birth
Enkidu (EN-kee-doo) Friend and companion of Gilgamesh
Atrahasis (ah-trah-HAH-sis) Mythological Babylonian king;
    also known as Utnapishtim

Gilgamesh and Enkidu

FROM THE DAY OF HIS BIRTH, Gilgamesh, king of Uruk, was singled out for glory. Part of him was divine, part mortal. His mother was the wise goddess Ninsun. His father was Lugalbanda, the heroic king who had held the throne before him.

Gilgamesh grew up strong, tall, and handsome. No one could match his skill with weapons or his courage in battle. In his youth he built the mighty walls of Uruk and the majestic temple of Inanna. But the young king was as arrogant as he was powerful. Like a wild bull, he lorded it over the people. He challenged the young nobles to violent games day and night,

> GILGAMESH WAS SINGLED OUT FROM THE DAY OF HIS BIRTH, TWO-THIRDS OF HIM WAS DIVINE, ONE-THIRD OF HIM WAS HUMAN!
> — THE EPIC OF GILGAMESH

knowing that he could beat them. He stole innocent daughters from their fathers and loving brides from their husbands.

Finally, the people of Uruk asked An for relief from their oppressive ruler. The great god called for Nintu, the birth goddess who had made the first man and woman. "You must create a new mortal," An told the goddess. "Make a hero with strength and courage equal to that of Gilgamesh. Let the two rivals fight each other, so the people of Uruk may have peace."

So Nintu pinched off a piece of clay and cast it over the open country. The clay sprang to life as Enkidu the warrior. Enkidu was a bull of a man. He had shaggy hair all over his body. He roamed the plains with the wild animals. Like a beast himself, he grazed on grass with the gazelles and drank at the water holes beside the wild cattle.

One day a hunter encountered Enkidu at a water hole. The young man stood stock-still with terror. Then he slowly crept away to the palace. When Gilgamesh heard the hunter's tale, his heart quickened. At last, the gods had sent him a worthy rival! "Go, hunter," the king commanded, "and take a priestess from Inanna's temple with you. Let her teach this mighty man-beast the ways of humans."

Off went the hunter, taking a priestess with him. Together they sat down by the water hole. When Enkidu came to drink, the woman enticed him with her charms. The savage man embraced her. Then he turned to rejoin his herd. But the wild beasts who had been his companions fled at the sight of him. When Enkidu tried to run too, he found that he could no longer keep up with them.

Sad and bewildered, Enkidu returned to the priestess. Taking his hand, the woman spoke to him gently. "You are no longer an untamed savage," she told Enkidu. "You have lost your innocence, but in return you have gained understanding. Come, I will take you to Uruk, where Gilgamesh alone is your equal."

As the woman spoke, Enkidu felt a sudden yearning to see the great walled city and the king who was its master. Leaving behind his wild life, he followed the priestess to Uruk. When the mighty warrior entered the city, a crowd gathered around him. "Look how strong he is," the people marveled. "At last a hero has come to challenge Gilgamesh!"

That night the king walked to the temple. He found Enkidu standing at the gate, blocking his path. "I am the strongest man in all the land!" bellowed the shaggy-haired warrior. "I was born on the grassy plains and raised on the milk of wild beasts! No one can stand before me!"

Outraged at the man's insolence, Gilgamesh challenged Enkidu to a fight. Like two raging bulls, the heroes clashed. The fury of their battle

> GILGAMESH AND ENKIDU GRAPPLED EACH OTHER,
>
> HOLDING FAST LIKE WRESTLERS,
>
> THEY SHATTERED THE DOORPOST, THE WALL SHOOK!
>
> ⌐ *THE EPIC OF GILGAMESH*

shook the walls of the temple and shattered the doorposts. Finally, Gilgamesh pinned his opponent. As he released Enkidu, he found that his anger had left him. In its place was joy, for at last he had found a worthy companion.

Enkidu stood and bowed in respect. "Hail to you, Gilgamesh," he said. "Truly you are the son of a goddess. Heaven itself has set you upon the throne. Long may you tower like a giant over your people!"

Then the two heroes embraced each other and became the closest of friends.

The Quest for Immortality

LIKE ALL HEROES, Gilgamesh and Enkidu loved adventure. Together they traveled across the land, fighting monsters. They killed Humbaba, the fire-breathing guardian of the Cedar Mountain. They vanquished the ferocious Bull of Heaven. But their brave deeds came to a tragic end. The gods decreed that Enkidu must die for his part in the slaughter of these sacred creatures.

After Enkidu's death, Gilgamesh was overcome with grief. He paced back and forth, tearing his hair and roaring like a wounded lion. He had lost his closest friend, the noble companion who had hunted and fought, laughed and wept beside him. With the loss a chilling fear

ENKIDU'S DREAM

The ancient Mesopotamians believed that dreams could foretell the future. In *The Epic of Gilgamesh*, Enkidu tells his friend about the terrifying dream he had after the two heroes killed the Bull of Heaven. Enkidu would fall ill the day after his dream and die twelve days later.

My friend, what a dream I had last night!

Heaven cried out, earth made reply,

I was standing between them.

There was a certain man, his face was somber,

His face was like that of the lion-headed monster-bird . . . ,

His hands were the paws of a lion,

His fingernails were the talons of an eagle.

He seized me by the hair, he was too strong for me,

I hit him but he sprang back like a swing rope,

He hit me and capsized me like a raft.

Like a wild bull he trampled me. . . .

Holding me fast, he took me down to the house of shadows, the dwelling of hell,

To the house whence none who enters comes forth,

On the road from which there is no way back,

To the house whose dwellers are deprived of light,

Where dust is their fare and their food is clay. . . .

There dwelt . . . the queen of the underworld, Ereshkigal.

[The] scribe of the netherworld . . . was kneeling before her,

She was holding a tablet and reading to her,

She lifted her head, she looked at me:

"Who brought this man?"

Above: Gilgamesh mourns the death of his bull-like friend Enkidu.

had settled in his heart. For the first time, the young king confronted the knowledge that one day he too must die.

Finally, Gilgamesh made a bold resolve. He would go in search of Atrahasis, the renowned king who had survived the great flood. Atrahasis was said to hold the secret of immortality. Perhaps he would teach Gilgamesh how to avoid the terrible fate that had befallen Enkidu.

For many days Gilgamesh traveled across the open country. At last he came to the edge of the world. There he saw a huge mountain with twin peaks that touched the heavens and roots that reached down to the underworld. Each night the sun passed through the mountain's long tunnel before rising again the next morning. The gate of the tunnel was guarded by the Scorpion-men. When Gilgamesh saw these deadly monsters, he nearly turned back in terror. But he gathered his courage and confronted them. And when the guardians saw that the king was determined to complete his quest, they agreed to open the gate of the mountain to him.

The quest for immortality brought the king to a passage guarded by the Scorpion-men.

At the first light of dawn, Gilgamesh entered the tunnel. He ran without stopping, for he knew that he would be burned alive if he remained in the tunnel when the sun entered it at nightfall. On and on the valiant king raced through the darkness. After twelve long hours, he emerged. He was in a garden of glittering jewels, and the sun still burned in the heavens.

A ferryman carries Gilgamesh across the Waters of Death.

Beyond the garden lay an immense sea. Gilgamesh persuaded an aged boatman to ferry him across the waters. For three days they traveled. At last the boat reached the distant home of Atrahasis, at the source of the rivers.

"Who are you, and why have you come here?" asked the immortal king.

"I am Gilgamesh, ruler of Uruk. Long have I journeyed across plains and mountains and waters to find you. My beloved friend Enkidu died and turned to clay. Teach me your secret, so that I may escape his fate."

"All things on earth must come to an end," said Atrahasis. Then the king told Gilgamesh the story of the great flood. The gods alone had saved him from destruction in that catastrophe. By the will of the gods, he and his wife would dwell on this distant isle forever. It was true that Atrahasis would never die, but he possessed no secret knowledge of immortality.

"The gods have made you king of a great city," the wise old man told Gilgamesh. "They have granted you strength and courage, love and friendship, dancing and merriment. Cease your pointless striving for life everlasting, and enjoy the life that you have been given."

Gilgamesh's eyes filled with tears. His long quest had ended in failure. When the wife of Atrahasis saw his despair, she asked her husband to give the hero a gift for his homeward journey. So the wise king told Gilgamesh about a prickly plant that grew deep beneath the water. Whoever ate this magical plant would become young again. He would not live forever, but he would remain youthful and strong all the days of his life.

Eagerly the hero turned to his new quest. He tied heavy stones to his feet and plunged into the sea. Sinking down to the bottom, he grabbed hold of the plant, although it pricked his hands until his blood reddened the waters. Then he cut the rope holding the stones and drifted back to the surface.

With the precious plant in his arms, Gilgamesh began the long journey back to Uruk. He crossed over the sea and passed through the mountain. He walked across the open country. At length he made camp beside a pool of clear water. As he bathed his weary body, a snake slithered out from the pool and ate the magical plant. The king wept as he watched the serpent shed its scaly skin, regaining its youth. After all his toil and trouble, he would return home empty-handed.

At last came the day when Gilgamesh beheld fair Uruk in the distance. How mighty were its walls! How strong its foundation! He had not achieved immortality, but the world would long remember the great king who had built this splendid city. For many years to come, Gilgamesh would rule the land in wisdom and compassion. And the story of his heroic adventures would live on long after death took him to join his friend Enkidu.

GLOSSARY

archaeologists scientists who study the physical remains of past cultures to learn about human life and activity

Assyrian relating to the people or culture of the Assyrian Empire, which was based in northern Mesopotamia. The Assyrians dominated Mesopotamia from the mid-fourteenth to early seventh centuries BCE.

Babylonian relating to the city-state of Babylon in southern Mesopotamia or to the Babylonian Empire. The Babylonians dominated Mesopotamia from the late eighteenth to mid-fourteenth centuries BCE and from the early seventh century to 539 BCE.

city-states independent states made up of a city and its surrounding territory

cuneiform (KYOO-nee-uh-form) a system of writing made up of characters formed from wedge-shaped strokes

epic a long narrative poem celebrating the deeds of legendary or historical beings

lapis lazuli a deep blue stone used in Mesopotamian jewelry and other treasures, which was considered the most beautiful and valuable of all stones

legend a traditional story that may involve ordinary mortals as well as divine beings and may be partly based on real people and events

me (pronounced *may*) the god-given rules and regulations that were believed to form the basis of human civilization

mythology the whole body of myths belonging to a people

myths traditional stories about gods and other divine beings, which were developed by ancient cultures to explain the mysteries of the physical and spiritual worlds

patron god a deity who was believed to be a city's special protector

personal god a god or goddess chosen by an individual as a sort of "guardian angel"

sage an extremely wise person

sanctuary a sacred place, which may be part of a temple or other religious building

scepter (SEP-ter) a staff carried by a king as a symbol of authority

scribes educated people who kept records, wrote out royal proclamations and laws, and performed other writing tasks for a living

shrine a place built for the worship of a god or goddess

silt small particles of earth deposited by water

Sumerian relating to the people, culture, or language of Sumer, the area in southern Mesopotamia that was the site of the world's first civilization

tamarisk a desert tree or shrub with feathery branches and pale green leaves

vizier (vih-ZEER) a high-ranking counselor to a king

ziggurats tall pyramid-shaped structures with a shrine at the top

ANCIENT MESOPOTAMIAN WRITING *and* TEXTS

More than five thousand years ago, Sumerian temple officials invented a set of symbols to keep track of goods produced, wages paid, gifts received, and other business. Eventually their simple markings developed into the complicated system of writing known as cuneiform. Cuneiform was composed of hundreds of different wedge-shaped characters, which were inscribed on clay tablets with a blunt instrument called a stylus.

Cuneiform characters on a Sumerian clay tablet

Professional scribes used cuneiform to record texts such as royal proclamations, government records, laws, business contracts, and private letters. The Mesopotamians also wrote down hymns, myths, epics, and other types of literary texts. Archaeologists have discovered thousands of inscribed clay tablets in the ruins of long-buried Mesopotamian cities. The oldest texts are recorded in Sumerian. Later texts are written in Akkadian, the language of the Babylonians and Assyrians.

The myths retold in this book are based mainly on the following sources:

"When on High"

This Babylonian creation story is based on the long poem *Enuma Elish,* also known as the *Babylonian Epic of Creation.* The earliest written version of *Enuma Elish,* dating back to around 1000 BCE, comes from seven clay tablets found in the ruins of King Assurbanipal's library at Nineveh. In another "edition," discovered in the Assyrian capital of Assur, the god Assur takes the place of Marduk as creator of the world.

"The Rebellion of the Gods" and "The Great Flood"

The Babylonian poem *Atrahasis* presents a mythological history of the human race, from the rebellion of the gods and the creation of the first men and women through the great flood sent to destroy humanity. *Atrahasis* may have been composed as early as the nineteenth century BCE. One of the earliest surviving copies, dating back to the seventeenth century BCE, was discovered in the ancient city of Sippar, near present-day Baghdad.

"Adapa and the South Wind"

In the myth of Adapa, a sage sent to earth by Enki passes up the chance to become immortal. This brief tale has been pieced together from fragments of clay tablets found at several ancient sites, including King Assurbanipal's library at Nineveh and an ancient government office at El-Amarna in Egypt. The oldest known copy dates back to the fourteenth century BCE.

"Inanna Descends to the Underworld"

The myth of Inanna's descent to the underworld is told in about four hundred lines of Sumerian text pieced together from fragments of about thirty clay tablets. Most of the tablets were inscribed around 1700 BCE and recovered from the ruins of the ancient Sumerian city of Nippur. Later versions, written in Akkadian, have been found at various Babylonian and Assyrian sites, including King Assurbanipal's library at Nineveh. Our retelling of the myth combines segments from several different versions.

"The Epic of Gilgamesh"

The Epic of Gilgamesh is one of the world's oldest major works of literature. It tells the adventures of Gilgamesh, semi-divine king of Uruk. Many different versions of this ancient tale have been found, dating back as early as 2100 BCE. The most complete version, often called the "standard version," is inscribed on eleven clay tablets found in King Assurbanipal's library at Nineveh.

To FIND OUT MORE

BOOKS

Bertman, Stephen. *Handbook to Life in Ancient Mesopotamia*. New York: Oxford University Press, 2003.

Davis, Kenneth C. *Don't Know Much about World Myths*. New York: HarperCollins, 2005.

Foster, Karen Polinger. *The City of Rainbows: A Tale from Ancient Sumer*. Oakville, CT: David Brown, 1999.

Hamilton, Virginia. *In the Beginning: Creation Stories from around the World*. San Diego, CA: Harcourt Brace Jovanovich, 1988.

Matthews, Rupert. *Myths and Civilization of the Ancient Mesopotamians.* Columbus, OH: Peter Bedrick Books, 2001.

McCaughrean, Geraldine. *Gilgamesh the Hero.* Grand Rapids, MI: Eerdmans Books for Young Readers, 2002.

Nardo, Don. *Empires of Mesopotamia.* San Diego, CA: Lucent Books, 2001.

Schomp, Virginia. *Ancient Mesopotamia: The Sumerians, Babylonians, and Assyrians.* New York: Scholastic, 2004.

Service, Pamela F. *Mesopotamia.* New York: Marshall Cavendish, 1999.

WEB SITES

Encyclopedia Mythica: Mesopotamian Mythology at
http://www.pantheon.org/areas/mythology/middle_east/mesopotamian
This online encyclopedia offers more than two hundred brief articles on the gods, goddesses, heroes, and demons of ancient Mesopotamia.

Gateways to Babylon at
http://www.gatewaystobabylon.com
Click on "Myths and Knowledge" for modern retellings of several ancient Mesopotamian myths. The site also includes an extensive glossary of Mesopotamian terms (see the "Religion and Magic" link), plus extracts from poems, hymns, and other ancient texts.

Mesopotamia at
http://www.mesopotamia.co.uk/menu.html
This excellent site from the British Museum includes lots of useful information on writing, religion, and other aspects of Mesopotamian society. Click on "Gods, Goddesses, Demons and Monsters" for a retelling of an ancient Mesopotamian creation story and information relating to the gods and other divine beings.

Mesopotamia: Sumer, Babylon, Assyria at
http://ancienthistory.mrdonn.org/AncientSumer.html
This easy-to-read site is presented by teachers Lin and Don Donn for teachers and students from kindergarten through grade twelve. The section on *The Epic of Gilgamesh* includes an interactive digital library book plus students' retellings of the story.

Mesopotamian Mythology at
http://www.godchecker.com/pantheon/mesopotamian-mythology.php
Godchecker is an online encyclopedia with a great sense of humor!
The site includes an introduction to Mesopotamian mythology plus
lively articles on more than seventy gods and goddesses.

SELECTED BIBLIOGRAPHY

Dalley, Stephanie. *Myths from Mesopotamia: Creation, the Flood, Gilgamesh, and Others.* Oxford, England: Oxford University Press, 1992.

Foster, Benjamin R. *Before the Muses: An Anthology of Akkadian Literature.* 3rd ed. Bethesda, MD: CDL Press, 2005.

———. *The Epic of Gilgamesh.* New York: W. W. Norton, 2001.

A seventh-century BCE tablet inscribed with part of *The Epic of Gilgamesh.*

Hallo, William W., and K. Lawson Younger Jr., eds. *The Context of Scripture.* 3 vols. Boston, MA: Brill Academic Publishers, 2003.

Kramer, Samuel Noah. *Sumerian Mythology.* New York: Harper and Row, 1961.

Kramer, Samuel Noah, ed. *Mythologies of the Ancient World.* Garden City, NY: Doubleday, 1961.

Kramer, Samuel Noah, and the editors of Time-Life Books. *Cradle of Civilization.* New York: Time-Life Books, 1967.

Nemet-Nejat, Karen Rhea. *Daily Life in Ancient Mesopotamia.* Westport, CT: Greenwood Press, 1998.

New Larousse Encyclopedia of Mythology. New York: Prometheus Press, 1974.

Rosenberg, Donna. *World Mythology: An Anthology of the Great Myths and Epics.* Lincolnwood, IL: Passport Books, 1986.

Snell, Daniel C. *Life in the Ancient Near East.* New Haven, CT: Yale University Press, 1997.

Wolkstein, Diane, and Samuel Noah Kramer. *Inanna: Queen of Heaven and Earth.* New York: Harper and Row, 1983.

NOTES ON QUOTATIONS

Quoted passages in sidebars come from the following sources:

"Enki Blesses the World," page 45, translated by Samuel Noah Kramer, in *Sumerian Mythology* (New York: Harper and Row, 1961) and *The Sumerians* (Chicago: University of Chicago Press, 1963).

"After the Flood," page 52, and "Enkidu's Dream," page 80, translated by Benjamin R. Foster, in *The Epic of Gilgamesh* (New York: W. W. Norton, 2001).

"Inanna Takes the *Me*," page 60, translated by Samuel Noah Kramer, in *Sumerian Mythology* (New York: Harper and Row, 1961).

"The Joy of Sumer," page 72, translated and retold by Samuel Noah Kramer and Diane Wolkstein, in *Inanna: Queen of Heaven and Earth* (New York: Harper and Row, 1983).

INDEX

ABOUT *the* AUTHOR

VIRGINIA SCHOMP has written more than sixty titles for young readers on topics including dinosaurs, dolphins, occupations, American history, and ancient cultures. Ms. Schomp earned a Bachelor of Arts degree in English Literature from Penn State University. She lives in the Catskill Mountain region of New York with her husband, Richard, and their son, Chip.